The Yogini Panini

Vegan Sandwiches, Burgers, and Sides

Dawn Grey

The Yogini Panini
Vegan Sandwiches, Burgers, and Sides
Dawn Grey

Visit our website at www.newdawnkitchen.com

Library of Congress Cataloging-in-Publication Data

ISBN-13:
978-1453872635

ISBN-10:
1453872639

Printed in the United States of America

Acknowledgements

This is my fifth cookbook, and would not be possible without the encouragement of my readers of my previous four "New Dawn Kitchen: Gluten-Free, Vegan, and Easily Sugar-Free Desserts", "The Virtuous Vegan", "The Gluten-Free Vegan Italian", and "Cinco de Vegan".

The Daiya Cheese Company, for making the yummiest gluten-free, vegan cheeses on the planet. Thank you for featuring my Macaroni and Cheese recipe on your website.

To my ex-husband, Gary Shainheit, who told me when we first met in college that "you can turn anything into a sandwich, and it usually tastes better".

My husband, Mark, who once again endured the kitchen messes and never ending shopping visits.

Last but not least, to my feline friend, Twilight, aka Yogi Purrananda. We did it again. I really am going to take the time to write a book about you☺

Yogi Purrananda, in deep prayer

Table of Contents

To The Reader

This book was specifically designed for those who wish to incorporate a plant-based dairy-free diet into their lives without missing out on the many recipes they may have come to love.

As this is my fifth cookbook, I have a loyal following of readers and clients, and am very grateful and blessed by each and every one of you. My first four books were very "cookbook-y" focusing on recipes, the types of ingredients you needed to prepare the vegan and/or gluten-free, sugar-free meals, and that was about it. I kept the reasons why one should eat vegan to a minimum, after all, they already bought or received the book, so there is no need to convince them to adhere to the lifestyle. However, what I have omitted, and what my friends, family, and clients want me to share this time, is more about me and how adhering to a vegan, and mostly gluten-free and sugar-free diet changed my entire life.

Several months ago, a Facebook "friend" very negatively commented on one of my posts. It really opened up my eyes, not so much from her comments, but from the comments of several other friends (who actually know me in real life) said in response. Before going into cookbook writing, I was and still am a holistic health practitioner and educator. My emphasis has changed as I have learned and evolved, but I am a firm believer that our lives are what we make of it, what we declare about ourselves, and what we believe. At the time, there was a discussion, bordering on debate, about the pending healthcare changes in the US, the possibility of a national healthcare system, and whether the changes are a benefit or detriment to us citizens. My comment to those in distress, one person in particular, was truly from the heart. It was not written to create controversy, to generate attention, or to promote my business. It was simply shared because it is what I believed as a result of my life experience. So to that one particularly distressed "friend", I replied on my page to her comment-

"Food is our medicine, as well as our dis-ease. You have the power to heal right now, by eating as Nature intended, affirming health and not surrendering your power to the supposed cure that you take every day that you are still waiting to work".

Oh boy, did that create a frenzy! Her reply was truly a compliment:

"Easy for you to say! Looking at your photo, you have obviously never been sick or fat a day in your life! What nonsense you preach!"

Why thank you! While I am not intending to cause a protest of the medical industry or healthcare system, (well maybe just a bit) it is a fact that we do not have healthcare in this country, we have sickcare. No one goes to the doctor because they are healthy and seeks a little something to keep that going, they go when they are sick, when something doesn't feel right. We have illnesses today we did not have 100+ years ago. We have never had more drugs, diagnostic tests, treatment centers, or medical providers than we do today. We have also never had as many sick, disabled, and critically ill people who are mostly supporting the industry, and do not appear to be getting any better. So, what's the deal?

My belief is that we are no longer healthy as a society because we have denatured our food and given our power over to the fear of disease and not the promotion of health. Am I the only one who has noticed that the majority of our commercials in the US are about fast food and medications? Why, in a rather intelligent and educated society, have we have not put the pieces of the puzzle together? Is it because, overall, we would rather have our chili and eat it too, along with an antacid or two or three, than to not eat it at all. We think bigger is better and then wonder why we have never been fatter and poorer than ever. We have allowed our taste buds to enslave us. If we are not careful, not only will obesity be the norm, but we will be too sick to work, collecting disability, and then everyone will be on a state or federal healthcare plan as a result. Alas, you manifest your own fears from your focus on it. What you resist persists. Stop giving your focus on money on what you do not want, and take responsibility for what you do want. HEALTH.

My message is not to point the finger at any one industry, nor do I want them banned. And I am certainly not teasing anyone. I was by far the most teased person in my class, having been, well, so obese I barely fit in the desk. I have eaten all the wrong foods, given every excuse as to why I was heavy, or sick, and of course it cannot possibly have anything to do with those boxes of mac and cheese I was eating, because my skinny friends ate them, too, or that I was too inactive, or that I was fat because I was starving myself of real food and nutrients and opted for frozen, instant, deep fried, sugar-coated, or otherwise "food" so loaded with chemicals and preservatives that it would have been seen as trash in my grandfather's day and thrown out. I am a firm believer in free choice and believe no one should limit what we do to our bodies or put in our bodies. However, when the very foods we give it each and every day take away the quality of life for ourselves, our families, and even our planet, something has to give.

We need to change the way we act. We first need to make sure the information is readily available so people know the truth and can empower themselves. To make a real change, to truly transform, we need to change our thinking. We need to take our power back and stop letting our addictions and laziness get the best of us. We need more than a New Year's resolution. We really need to stop acting like spoiled 4 year olds and grow up.

I also am a firm believer that just about everyone who is overweight, sick, or somehow not yet feeling the effects of their poor choices (yet) know full well that they need to quit doing this to themselves. I know many people who drink unlimited coffee and energy drinks, then cannot sleep at night. Hence the next day begins with coffee and energy drinks. This is a vicious cycle.

For many, going vegan is synonymous with a life of living without rather than living with. It is also believed to be an inconvenience to have to actually spend an hour boiling up some brown rice when white rice is ready in 20, or that instant boil in a pouch product will give you "rice" in 3. We want our food fast, we want a huge amount of it, we want it cheap, and of course, we want it to taste good so we slather it in butter, salt, oil, cheese, cream, mayo, or whatever we want. Then, we want a diet pill to negate it. I don't think so.

What if I told you that you really did not need to give up anything but your aches, pains, poor health, and empty wallet? What if I told you that once I evaluated my food, my mood, and how I felt, and took the plunge and made the changes, I lost the weight AND the pre-diabetes, the high blood pressure, the high cholesterol, the need for doctors, drugs, drugs, and more drugs, and tests all the time to monitor my conditions, the asthma inhaler, the allergy shots, and the feeling the each and every time I woke up, stood up, or bent over that I was simply not going to be able to endure another moment of the day. What if I told you that I am several hundred dollars a month ahead by not having to run on the treadmill of pursuing sickcare?

We have become quite conditioned in mind and taste buds as to what constitutes a meal, myself included. I was not raised vegan in the least, and it showed in my weight and health as mentioned above. Well known to be the fat girl of my class, the standard American diet of meat, dairy, and oversized portions of salt, fat, and sugar expanded my waistline to the point I was nearly as wide as I was tall. When I was 8 years old, I had already hit 200 pounds. My waist was 44 inches and I was 58 inches tall. That's just not right, and blows the whole BMI chart of the wall. I cannot say I was eating any more than my friends, at least at first, but what I ate stuck to me and weighed on me, literally. When you are fat and feel you cannot lose weight, you quit trying and just gorge- at least I did.

I have gained and lost weight significantly three times in my life, so I have learned a thing or two about what it means to be fat, be thin, and be on a diet. Luckily I am off of that rollercoaster. When I say I lost 170 pounds, I do not mean scattered over my lifetime, but at one time, because I dieted myself to over 300 pounds using a very popular diet plan that I paid to attend weekly meetings and bought many of their products in the store. Once again, fat AND poor. I hit rock bottom, fearing I would either explode from a heart attack or blood pressure that went too high, but also because my premiums for insurance was too high and I could not pay them- I lost my policy, did not qualify for medical assistance, and would therefore be suddenly and totally without my so-called "cures". At the time, my job did not offer insurance. I really thought I was going to die. I see now I most certainly was, but from my own diet and actions and not necessarily lack of healthcare.

I did what many Americans do when they can no longer afford their medicines- I began to research alternative medicine. This brought me to a local health food store. After flipping through numerous books and magazines, and being quite intimidated by products (what is Kohlrabi and what exactly do you do with it?), I almost walked out. Lucky for me, a smiling person approached me, who looked healthy and glowing, and she could tell I was out of my element. I never got her name, but she said something that stays with me today,

"If it's dead, it does not promote life. If it grows, it does."

That is all she said. That is all she needed to. I connected the dots to my pizza parties, my double cheeseburgers, even my lower fat grilled chicken sandwiches with fat-free yogurt, skim milk, and diet products galore. While many debate if humans should eat meat or milk, (and I truly have an opinion on this now) we certainly agree that fat-free cookies do not grow on trees. What health benefit is there of a breakfast of donuts and coffee? Who decided it's OK and acceptable to have a breakfast of eggs, bacon, and pancakes that look more like a triple decker dessert than a meal? Maybe, just maybe, I am supposed to eat some living food?

I bought some leafy green things (but left the Kohlrabi alone), some "fake meat" products, and a magazine at the checkout stands. I learned that while it took some getting used to, especially as far as preparation goes, it was not as bad as I thought. Most of it was quite tasty. I felt full after eating, not bloated or guilty. True I do not like every single vegetable in existence, and some meals were disasters, but I never liked every single cut of meat, either and certainly charred a steak or two in my day.

I discovered that plant-based foods are delicious when you find the right recipes, are cheaper, and in my case, eliminated every single health condition, including my weight problem. So, I went from being fat and sick and poor to being energetic, leaner and in such good health that someone who never knew me before could say,

> "Easy for you to say! Looking at your photo, you have obviously never been sick or fat a day in your life! What nonsense you preach!"

Thank you for the compliment, anonymous Facebook friend. You have solidified my comment I had posted and brought to my attention why this book needed to speak a bit more about my past rather than just my academic and work credentials to write such books to begin with. I am living proof, and I have many high school and college friends whom I still stay in touch with to verify my story, that I was the fat kid who missed on average 40 days of school a year, and now I am the employee who has one of the best attendance records and doesn't look anywhere near her age. I did nothing magical and nothing you cannot do. I just ate real food.

It is my belief that while food is fuel, it is meant to be enjoyed and celebrated. There is no reason to ever eat something you do not like, nor do I believe you should ever eat food that taste less than delicious. For those, like me, who are suddenly presented with an immediate reason to give up an entire food group or two, I know this can create quite a challenge. I also know it's an adventure and a blessing in disguise. This is the chance to gain your freedom.

Besides, eating vegan (which means abstaining from meat, dairy, and eggs, as well as animal derived products such as honey if you want to take it to that level) can be tasty. For dinner I ate eggplant Parmesan on ciabatta bread, with a roast vegetable salad, and Mozzarella sticks and minestrone soup as appetizers and ended with cheesecake. Yeah, being vegan is terrible, isn't it? ☺

Believe me, with some curiosity and patience, you will discover, like me, that you can recreate almost every one of your favorite meals that have less than favorable side effects. I grew up Italian, so that explains my dinner. Your comfort food may be any number of dishes, perhaps Lasagna or Mexican. I have cookbooks specializing in both of those cuisines, as well as a dessert book. There is no suffering in being vegan if you are willing to change your mind about it. My books will help you, and there are many wonderful new products to give you the convenience of fast food with far less impact on your health and waistline.

This cookbook, The Yogini Panini, was requested by those who missed sandwiches and burgers. Americans so love their burgers! In fact, over the last 12 years of working as a holistic health consultant, my clients, who realize they needed to go vegan to save their lives and this planet, asked me how I gave up burgers. Since moving to Kansas, that is what they do not want to give up. In the New York Metro area where I was raised, more often than not, it was "how do you give up cheese (mostly in Italian food). I simply would give them a recipe and tell them this is how I did it. Now, they did it too. And with this book, you can as well.

Do not fool yourself- a vegan style burger will not seem so much like meat that you will not know the difference. In the end, I know at any time, if I really want a beef burger, I can have it. It is not off limits. But in embracing a more healthful lifestyle, I became more conscious of how I feel emotionally and spiritually. Now, I simply do not want to harm my body, an animal, and the environment because I want that slab of beef. What I missed was being able to have a burger-like meal, especially when hosting a party or gathering with friends. I liked the comfort and convenience of hot and cold sandwiches, which so many of us see as the stereotypical lunch.

I practice Yoga, both the exercise and philosophy, and they have a principle called Ahimsa, non-violence. In walking the path of better health, I developed a stronger connection with my body and my place in the Universe. I personally believe the harm I inflict on the animal ultimately creates the harm in my body. I am not here to convert anyone, or create a group of readers with a guilty conscience, but that is where I am at in my mindset today. I want you, too, to explore what practices harm you, and which ones restore you, and listen to that. Ahimsa is something even a non-yogi can and should consider each day, all day long. Hence, the Yogini Panini.

For those of you who have read any of my other 4 cookbooks, you will notice this book is gluten-free friendly, but is not exclusively gluten-free like the other 4. I will carefully note which ones are or can convert to gluten-free with a (GF) after the title. Those recipes that need a modification *other* than swapping a bread product will have an (*) next to ingredients that need substituting, and suggestions at the end of the recipe.

For those readers who do not know what gluten-free is, you may want to consider yourself lucky. Gluten is the protein that occurs in many grains. As much as 10% of the population is unable to ingest gluten without having some very uncomfortable side effects. I myself cannot tolerate bleached, refined white flour products, and restrict gluten most of the year.

There is also extensive research being done to connect gluten (as well as the milk protein casein) to being a factor in ADHD, autism, schizophrenia, depression, fibromyalgia, and chronic fatigue. I myself will tell you that when I ate refined bleached flour, I ached from head to toe and had what I thought was the beginning of inflammatory bowel disease. I removed bleached white flour, limited all other intake of gluten, and have not had a flare up of either condition since.

Please note, my gluten-free pals, that I have not abandoned your cause! Keep in mind, I too get affected if I am not careful. Rather, I wanted to expand the reach of my vegan crowd and create sandwich recipes that would most mimic and comfort the newbie. As such, several recipes included rely on prepackaged goods that have wheat or gluten. However, there are still many options here for you, and if you can find equivalent products that happen to be gluten-free, I most certainly want you to use them. Remember, my selection of bread recipes is at the end of the book if you cannot obtain what you need locally.

The last chapter of the book offers some bread recipes reprinted from my book, "The Virtuous Vegan" for those who have difficulty obtaining gluten-free breads, or those who want to give gluten-free bread baking a try.

Remember always, to enjoy your food. If you do not care for my selection of vegetables, beans, or bread, simply switch to those you will like. My goal is to empower you with more choices for eating and cooking.

Namaste,

Dawn Grey

Introduction

Dairy Products: To Eat Or Not To Eat

While most of us are familiar with lactose intolerance and milk allergies, there are other reasons why more and more individuals are reducing or eliminating dairy from their diets. In this age of environmental awareness, using plant-based milk substitutes is more popular due to their smaller impact on environmental waste. Also, for those who are concerned about animal cruelty, avoiding milk helps reduce factory farming practices. Since most dairy cows are supplied with antibiotics, hormones, and fed food that is laced with pesticides, it may be best if we all took a step away from dairy.

For those of you who are (turning) vegan (choose to eliminate all animal products), dairy allergic, or lactose intolerant, follow the recipes using whatever milk or cheese substitute you wish. You will also find that some recipes call for yogurt, cheese, and/or sour cream. For convenience I will call these "milk product", "vegan sour cream", "non-dairy yogurt " and "vegan cheese" the first time, and from there, just yogurt, milk, etc. If you bought this book because of your gluten/wheat sensitivity and are not following a dairy-free guideline, feel free to use whatever dairy products you wish in equal measure.

I want to take a moment to discuss the flavor of non-dairy products. If you are very new to dairy alternatives, please note that not all dairy-free milks, cheeses, and other products taste the same. While most would say that they could not tell the difference between one brand of 2% milk from another, I assure you there is major variety in texture, flavor, sweetness, etc. between rice and soy milk, and even among the individual brands of soy milk. Be patient, try many brands, and stick with what you love. For me, I really had a hard time with the vegan cheeses, as casein, a common ingredient in dairy-free cheeses, is actually a milk protein, and hence, not dairy-free. The first time I discovered this, I shot out a nasty email to a company, claiming they were falsely advertising their soy cheese, and that if I had wanted dairy, I would have saved $3 and bought real cheese. They apologized, and a week later, a drop shipment of numerous bags of their assorted shredded cheeses were on my doorstep. At first I was really angry, as I made it clear that I am so sensitive to dairy that I get high fevers (105°F) and often need hospitalization if I had more than an accidental taste. I had just recovered from such an episode that luckily I was able to heal from at home, and I felt this really showed their inability to understand that dairy means anything that comes from milk from an animal. Lactose and casein and whey are all different dairy by-products and you can be highly allergic to casein and not be lactose intolerant.

So I stayed away from all cheese, even the truly vegan ones because those that did not have casein tasted like slippery plastic. And then one day I found Daiya cheese online, and my ability to cook and eat my favorite mac and cheese, lasagna, and everything else was restored. Even my husband will eat Daiya cheese. I made a pot of my macaroni and cheese for the 4th of July and those that ate it did not know. I actually took it to be a major compliment when my sister-in-law said it "tasted like Velveeta" because until now, there was no vegan cheese that could fool the taste buds.

I must stress that I am not affiliated with any of the brands I should mention in these pages, but in some cases, like Daiya, there was no other alternative (in my opinion) that even came close, and until their emergence, that chapter of my cooking experience was closed. Now, it's re-opened. This book would not exist without those few companies who went out of their way to cater to those of us who cannot or will not consume the traditional products.

Fats: The Good, The Bad, And The Ugly

Remember when margarine first came out and we thought it was healthful to smear gobs of it on our food to get the healthful polyunsaturated fats? Well, like most other food trends, the good and the bad fats list keeps getting updated. Here is my take on fats, as far as this cookbook is concerned: use what is readily available to you. While I am the first to say NO to traditional shortening and lard, if you prefer these, then use them. True they are bad for you, but let's be honest- unless you have an extreme food problem, even the most rich and decadent meal eaten in moderation and not on a daily basis should be fine for your health and your waistline. However, I am the first to say that I love good food, and overindulged a few too many times in the writing of this book.

The main fat most of us need to substitute in dairy-free and vegan cooking is butter. Butter in many ways may actually be healthier than the trans fats in most margarines, but for those who cannot or will not have dairy, both products are likely unsafe to use. My suggestion for recipes that really need a "stick" of butter is to use vegan brands such as "Earth Balance". The buttery blend one is quite tasty on gluten-free toast, but again, fat is fat, so a little goes a long way.

The newest "fat" to get attention these days is coconut oil. Coconut oil is reported to have antibiotic and even weight loss benefits when used moderately. Use common sense. Tablespoons of fat of any kind is not a weight loss tonic, but having the right essential fats in the right quantities is healthful. Some brands are pricier than others, but I have learned that the higher the price, usually the better the buttery flavor. The lower priced ones in general smell and taste like coconut, so keep this in mind. Some desserts and vegetables taste wonderful with this coconut flavor, whereas other recipes, such as beans, it is just too overpowering, so a higher grade of coconut oil is needed.

Therefore when I bake cakes and prepare recipes that require a lot of oil, I rely on canola, or olive oil if it does not require heating. If you prefer another oil besides olive or canola oil, simply substitute that oil for the butter or oil called for in a recipe.

Want To Reduce Fat?

While our recipes will be naturally cholesterol-free because we have omitted all animal products, almost all of our recipes contain oil, margarine, cheese, or all. However, most are considered low-fat compared to their original. For those of you who need or want to reduce the fat even more, there are a number of substitutions you can use.

One of the most popular ways to reduce fat is to use less oil and more water to sauté in. My overall suggestion is to use less cooking oil, less oil in dressings, and more broth, vinegar, water, or non-fat liquids whenever possible. You can also go lighter on the cheese, sour cream, etc. I would prefer to just eat a smaller portion of something cheesy and higher in fat, like the eggplant Parmesan sandwich, and then fill up on a low fat salad or soup than not have it at all. Moderation is still the best diet.

Egg-Free Cooking

If you are vegan or cannot consume eggs or egg yolks like me, you have several options to use as substitutes. Unlike swapping oils and milk for another product, not every egg substitute will work for every recipe, so removing eggs from a recipe is perhaps just as tricky, if not more so, than making the gluten-free switch. For this cookbook, we reference a product called Egg Replacer, a powder sold in most health food markets.

Peanut Free/Nut Free

For a nut-free peanut butter substitute try using sunflower seed butter, commonly found as the product "Sunbutter" in recipes. Sesame seed butter (also called tahini) is another choice, but requires (in my opinion) a touch of liquid sweetener to offset its savory taste. Other seed and nut butters include macadamia nut butter, cashew butter, pecan butter, and my favorite, almond butter. You may want to sweetener or salt the recipe differently depending on your like for salt and sweet. You can also use soy nuts in recipes or for snacks in equal measure as you would use other nuts.

Limiting Sodium

While the body does need some sodium, we are being overloaded terribly in this country with the amount that makes its way into our food supply. There are a number of potassium salt products out there for those who must watch their sodium intake. Spices and salt-free spice blends really wake up vegetables and beans, and I honestly like the potassium salts to help reduce the sodium count in recipes like my Unfries. Feel free to use in equal measure or less, as potassium salt, as far as I am concerned, seems more salty and concentrated.

What is Gluten?

As mentioned earlier, gluten is the protein that naturally occurs in the following grains: wheat, rye, barley, durum, semolina, einkorn, graham, bulgur, couscous, spelt, farro, kamut, and triticale. Commercial oats also contain gluten due to cross contamination in processing, but actually are gluten-free otherwise. Depending on your level of sensitivity will depend if you can use regular oats or if you need to invest in oats that specifically indicate they are gluten-free. I myself am not sensitive enough for the cross-contamination of oats, so I buy regular oats, which are more affordable and certainly easier to obtain. I would consult with your healthcare provider or nutritionist as to whether or not you can handle oats, or any product for that matter, that is processed on equipment or manufactured in the same environment, as a gluten product.

Therefore, gluten will be present in these grains flours and byproducts, such as barley malt, beer, and many flavorings and spices. Gluten is in soy sauce, MSG, and many condiments. It is also in just about every prepackaged vegan "cold cut" and protein product available that I have found. Please read your labels if gluten is off limits. However, living gluten-free is not a death sentence. I have baked cookies, breads, cakes, and just about everything else with a gluten-free flour or blend of flours. They cost more, but you will need to take less days off of work because of tummyaches, bowel issues, and other nasties. You can buy gluten-free bread, pizza dough, and everything imaginable these days.

What Grains and Flours are Gluten-Free?
Corn flour, cornmeal, and cornstarch
Buckwheat and buckwheat flour
Rice flour- white and brown
Quinoa, quinoa cereal flakes, and quinoa flour
Millet and millet flour
Sorghum flour
Amaranth and amaranth flour
Certified gluten-free oats and oatmeal
Coconut flour
Teff flour
Nut meals and flours- almond, chestnut, pecan, cashew
Garbanzo, fava bean, pea, soy and other bean flours
Tapioca pearls and tapioca starch/flour (they are the same product)
Potato starch
Potato flour (which is different than potato starch)
Sweet potato and yam flour
Arrowroot starch

Why Eat Wheat/Gluten-Free?

There is a growing awareness that a number of individuals experience mild to severe gastro-intestinal distress when eating wheat/gluten containing foods. While most individuals are more likely to have sensitivity to these foods if eaten in excess, there are those who have allergies to wheat or gluten and therefore cannot safely eat even a small portion of the culprit food.

Another concern is Celiac Disease, a condition in which a person is intolerant to gluten containing foods. In the body of someone with this condition, consuming gluten containing food sets off an autoimmune response that causes damage to the small intestine. This, in turn, causes the small intestine to lose the ability to absorb nutrients, leading to malnutrition, permanent intestinal damage, and possibility of requiring surgery.

There is a belief that removing gluten as well as casein, a protein found in dairy, helps children with Autism Spectrum Disorder. Some parents report improvements in autism symptoms with this dietary regimen. Little actual research has been done, however, on the gluten-free/casein-free diet for autism. However, since there is no dietary need for gluten or casein in the diet, so there is no harm in removing them if they help you or your child's health.

For those who find that eating wheat and/or gluten containing foods creates mild to moderate distress, it is recommended to follow an elimination diet and consult with a healthcare provider and/or dietician for further assistance.

Now, on to the best part- eating! For any recipe that offers a gluten-based protein, feel free to substitute lentils, sliced/diced Portabellas, or any other product you desire.

Panini

Panini are sandwiches, Italian in origin. In Italy, a panino (singular for panini) is customarily made from a small roll or loaf of bread, typically a ciabatta. The loaf is cut horizontally and filled with salami, ham, cheese, mortadella or other food. In Central Italy, there is a popular version of panino which is filled with porchetta, a type of sliced, roasted pork. (You won't find these recipes in here!) In the United States and the UK, panini are typically grilled or toasted and deviate from traditional coldcuts.

Some of our combinations are creative, others remakes of traditional sandwiches you thought you had to give up. Perhaps my ideas will inspire some of your own. In the words of my ex-husband, Gary, "you can turn anything into a sandwich, and its usually better". Taking the lead from Gary, turn the page.

Yogini Panini (GF)

My favorite sandwich, well before I was vegan, hence the name of the book. I love this with a baked sweet potato on the side.

1 medium zucchini, sliced
1 yellow squash, sliced
1 red pepper, sliced
3 artichoke hearts, fresh, frozen, or jarred
1 Portabella mushroom cap
1 red onion, sliced into rings
2 Tablespoons of hummus or other preferred bean dip
A pinch of oregano, basil, and garlic powder
Sundried tomatoes and shredded lettuce, optional
Vegan cheese, if desired, any variety
Sandwich bread- I prefer Ciabatta

Preheat oven to 450° F. Place sliced zucchini, yellow squash, pepper, artichoke hearts, and Portabella on a cookie sheet. Drizzle with oil or non-stick spray. Sprinkle with spices. Broil for 15 minutes, or until vegetables brown and reduce in size.

Spread hummus and cheese on bread. Assemble roasted vegetables on top, then add tomatoes, lettuce, and any other optional toppings.

Use a sandwich grill, pan, or Panini press to toast sandwich, or eat as is. Serve warm.

Eggless Salad (GF)

I never cared for traditional egg salad, or may for that matter, but every now and then, this really hits the spot.

2 Tablespoons vegan mayonnaise
1 Tablespoon sweet pickle relish
1 teaspoon distilled white vinegar
1 teaspoon prepared yellow mustard
½ teaspoon ground turmeric
1 Tablespoon dried parsley
1 pound firm tofu, sliced, pressed, and well drained
1 Tablespoon minced onion
2 Tablespoons minced celery
Salt and pepper, to taste

In a small bowl, combine mayonnaise, relish, vinegar, mustard, turmeric, and parsley. Mix well, and reserve.

In a separate bowl, mash tofu. Stir in the mayonnaise mixture. Add onion, celery, and salt and pepper.

Refrigerate at least one hour before serving.

Place drained tofu in large bowl, and crumble with a fork. Stir in onion and celery. Mix in reserved mixture. Season to taste with salt and pepper. Chill for several hours to allow flavors to blend.

Buffalo Tofu Wrap (GF)

1 pound of extra-firm tofu
½ cup hot sauce or already prepared buffalo sauce
¼ cup vegan butter
Garlic powder (optional)
Wrapper, Naan, Chapati, or other bread of choice

Press tofu under heavy weight for 30 minutes, such as a thick book or container. Sprinkle with garlic powder if desired.

Cut tofu into strips. Melt butter in a small saucepan over low heat. Reserve.

In a separate small frying pan, heat some butter or cooking spray. Fry the tofu over medium heat, being careful not to burn. When the first side is golden brown, flip over.

When the butter in the saucepan is melted, gently stir in the hot sauce with a wooden spoon. When the two are sufficiently mixed, pour sauce slowly over the tofu.

Vegan Chicken Salad (GF)

I used to get a premade version of this at a small healthfood store in New Jersey, and missed it once I moved away. It took some doing, but now, I have my own version (that I must admit is better!)

 1 cup tempeh, cubed
 ½ cup vegan mayonnaise
 1 celery, finely chopped
 1 medium pickle, finely chopped
 ½ of a medium onion, chopped
 2 Tablespoons parsley, minced
 1 teaspoon yellow mustard
 2 teaspoons wheat-free tamari

Steam tempeh in a bamboo steamer or other device for 7 minutes or until it begins to crumble.

Remove from heat and set aside. Toss together all ingredients.

Refrigerate at least one hour before serving.

Serve with your choice of bread.

Chicken Fried Chicken (GF)

So much better than the traditional fried slab of bird. Several of my taste testers who are not vegan and normally do not like tofu enjoyed these.

1 teaspoon salt
1 teaspoon onion powder
1 teaspoon garlic powder
1 teaspoon black pepper
1 ½ cups flour, regular or gluten-free*
¼ cup nutritional yeast
¼ cup prepared mustard
2 Tablespoons baking powder
½ cup water
1 pound of extra firm tofu, pressed
Oil for frying
Ciabatta or other heavy bread for sandwich making

In a large bowl, mix together the salt, onion powder, garlic powder, flour, black pepper, and nutritional yeast.

In a separate bowl, whisk together the mustard and water. Add ½ cup of the flour mixture to the mustard mixture and combine well. Add baking powder to the flour mixture and combine well.

Slice tofu in 4 pieces horizontally. Coat with the mustard, then coat each piece with the dry flour mixture.

Fry in the oil over medium-high heat in a large skillet for 3-5 minutes, until golden brown. Turn halfway during the cooking.

Drain on paper towels, serve with ketchup, mustard, vegan mayo, or your favorite sandwich condiments.

French Dip

Gluten-Free Idea: Use sliced Portabellas instead of the Steak strips

> 2 teaspoons cooking oil
> 1 medium bell green pepper, sliced into strips
> 1 medium yellow onion, sliced into strips
> 1 clove garlic, minced
> 1 package Lifeline Smart Strips® Steak
> Vegan Cheddar
> 2 sub rolls

> **Au Jus**
> 2 cups vegetable stock, unsalted
> 2 teaspoons vegan Worcestershire sauce (no anchovies)
> Black pepper to taste

Heat olive oil in over medium heat. Cook green pepper, garlic and yellow onion, stirring gently, until just tender.

Remove pepper and onion from heat and add steak slices to the pan. Cook about 3 minutes, just until hot, and remove from heat. If desired, season with salt and pepper to taste.

Make au jus: Place all ingredients in a small pot and heat, whisking occasionally, until hot. Remove from heat to serving dishes or bowls.

Assemble sandwiches by first adding the beef strips, followed by the peppers and onions. Top with cheese and serve bowls of au jus for dipping.

Chicken Caesar Sandwiches

Lightlife's sliced chicken strips may appear Gluten-free, but they have barley malt extract in the ingredients. If you are sensitive to gluten, you may not want to try them. As always, use tofu, tempeh, or sliced Portabellas instead.

1 package of Lightlife Smart Strips Chick'n®
½ cup of romaine lettuce
4 slices of tomato
2 Tablespoons of Ceaear dressing (recipe below)

Dressing
1 Tablespoon lemon juice
1 teaspoon vegetarian Worcestershire sauce
1 teaspoon onion powder
1 teaspoon Dijon mustard
1 garlic clove, minced
¼ cup olive oil
8 slices of bread for panini

Mix dressing ingredients and refrigerate.

Cook Chick'n strips in a small frying pan with a small amount of oil until warm, about 3-5 minutes.

Assemble sandwiches. Serve as is, or toast in panini press, griddle, or toaster oven if desired.

BBQ sandwiches (GF)

1 package of plain tempeh, cut into strips
2 Portabella mushroom caps, sliced
3 Tablespoons oil
2 Tablespoons wheat-free Tamari or soy sauce
2 teaspoons Dijon mustard
1 teaspoon garlic powder
Salt and pepper to taste
1 teaspoon maple syrup
Bread of choice

Preheat the oven to 350° F.

Make the marinade by combining the oil, tamari, mustard and salt and pepper in a small bowl. Brush both sides of the tempeh slices with the marinade and place on a lightly oiled baking sheet. Marinade tempeh and mushrooms for at least an hour.

Add maple syrup to the remaining marinade. Brush both sides of tempeh and mushrooms with marinade and place on another lightly oiled baking sheet.

 Place both baking sheets in the oven. After 15 minutes, flip tempeh slices over and continue cooking for another 15 minutes. Tempeh should be browned and tempeh should be browned and crisp at the end of cooking time. If you need to leave them in longer, you may do so. Let cool after removing from oven.

Assemble sandwiches and toast if desired.

Pear Cheese Melt (GF)

A simple sandwich for breakfast, lunch, or any time of day. For variety, substitute seasonal apples or a combination.

2 slices bread of choice
1 pear of your choice, sliced
2 slices of vegan cheese, any variety

Slice the pear into thin slices.

Place cheese slices over the pears.

Thinly coat a pan with vegetable oil or cooking spray.

Put the sandwich together and grill lightly on each side until cheese is melted. It melts better if you put a lid on the pan so the heat gets captured.

Cream Cheese and Olive Sandwich (GF)

This can be a stand alone sandwich, or used as a spread for other veggie based sandwiches or burgers.

½ cup shredded Daiya or other vegan Mozzarella cheese
¼ cup green olives, chopped
¼ cup black olives, chopped
A pinch of oregano
Sandwich bread of choice
Small amount of vegan cream cheese
1 marinated roasted red pepper

Spread cream cheese on two halves of bread. Sprinkle shredded cheese on top.

Place olives on top of the cream cheese, followed by the red pepper. Serve cold or grill if desired.

Day After Thanksgiving Panini

Now, vegans can have leftovers, too. Great with potato salad. Tofurky® is a readily available brand of vegan cold cut, made from soy and wheat protein.

5 slices Tofurky® deli slices, any flavor
1 Portabella mushroom, sliced into thin strips
2 slices bread
½ cup cranberry sauce, any variety
Vegan margarine/butter

Melt a small amount of butter in a frying pan over medium heat. When melted, put in the two slices of bread.   When the bread is browned, flip each slice over.

Add the Tofurky® slices on one piece. Smear a small amount of cranberry sauce on the other slice.

When warm, Press the sandwich together. Serve with mashed potatoes, baked fries, or other hearty side dish.

BBQ Portabella Sandwich (GF)

This is one of those sandwiches that anyone can enjoy that just so happens to be vegan and gluten-free if you choose the right bread.

2 large Portabella Mushrooms
3 Tablespoons of Oil
1 Tablespoon *each* oregano and basil
2 Tablespoon balsamic vinegar
2 cloves of garlic, minced
½ cup any leafy salad green of choice
Salt and pepper to taste
Roasted Sweet Red Peppers, fresh or from a jar
4 slices of your choice of bread

In a blender combine the oil, balsamic vinegar, garlic, salt, pepper, and herbs until the items are well blended.

Clean and discard the stem of the mushrooms and place in a bowl. Pour the marinade over the mushrooms and let soak for at least 30 minutes.

Heat a large frying pan over medium high heat. Add a small amount of oil or vegan butter to the pan, or brush mushrooms with oil to prevent sticking if using a grill. Cook the mushrooms and continue to baste during the cooking time. Save some marinade to top off your sandwich.

To build the sandwich place two or three leaves of greens on the bread, then add the roasted red pepper slices. Next, add the grilled mushrooms and add a bit of marinade. Top off with the other slice of bread and add optional cheese.

Gyro

Seitan, pronounced say-tan, is concentrated wheat gluten and is very high in protein. A definite no-no for the gluten intolerant, I suggest mushrooms if you would otherwise like to duplicate the gyro.

1 Tablespoon oil
1 package of unflavored seitan
4 Pita bread
1 cup shredded lettuce
1 cup sliced tomato
1cup chopped red onion

Cook seitan with oil over medium heat, 3-5 minutes.

Split the pitas bread in half to open.

Divide lettuce, tomato, onion, and seitan between the halves.

Fajita Wrap (GF)

Feel free to add tempeh, tofu, or other protein choices.

1 red pepper
1 green pepper
1 Portabella mushroom
1 zucchini
1 onion
Salt and pepper
¼ teaspoon of chili powder

Toppings
Shredded lettuce
Tomato
Vegan cheese, shredded
Salsa
Vegan sour cream
Wrappers or Naan, regular or gluten-free

Slice up vegetables into long strips. Add a little water to a frying pan and set heat at medium-high. Add salt and pepper to taste. Cook vegetables for 3-5 minutes, or until desired texture. Sprinkle with chili powder.

Add the vegetables (raw and cooked) into the bread product. Add desired toppings.

Tomato and Mozzarella Sandwich (GF)

This sandwich takes on a completely different flavored when grilled, but is equally good cold.

Bread of choice
1 teaspoon of olive oil
1 teaspoon of balsamic vinegar
¼ teaspoon of dried oregano
¼ cup shredded vegan Mozzarella cheese
1 large tomato, sliced
1 red onion, thinly sliced
A few leaves of fresh basil

Take two pieces of bread or a split open roll and drizzle one side of both with olive oil and vinegar. On same side sprinkle both with a generous amount of oregano. Place this side down in toaster oven or in a small frying pan.

Place the Mozzarella on the piece of bread on the side you did not apply oil. Cover the cheese with tomato slices, red onions, and fresh basil leaves.

If toasting, use Panini press or wrap in aluminum foil and pan fry for 1-2 minutes on each side to melt the cheese. Unwrap carefully.

BLT

All the flavor and fun of the traditional without the grease.

- 1 Tablespoon + 1 Tablespoon vegan margarine, divided
- 3 strips Lightlife Smart Bacon or other vegan brand
- 1 slice of vegan cheese, any flavor
- 2 slices bread
- 1 leaf romaine lettuce, sliced
- 3 slices tomato

In a small pan, melt margarine and cook bacon until it is the desired crispiness. Remove from heat and set aside.

Place ingredients all on the bread. Once assembled, add another pad of butter and grill. Serve with pickles or other sides.

Chipotle Chicken

2 slices bread of choice
1 package of Lightlife Smart Strips Chick'n®
½ cup of salsa
½ cup shredded vegan Cheddar cheese
1 ½ teaspoons chili powder, or to taste
2 Tablespoons softened vegan butter

Spread a small amount of butter on the bread and place face-down in pan or Panini press.

Spread the other side, face up, of each piece with the salsa.

Place the chicken strips on top of only one of the slices, and sprinkle with cheese and chili powder. Place the top piece of bread onto the sandwich.

Cook until the bread is crispy and golden brown, and flip over. Sandwich should be done in 3-5 minutes total, when the cheese is melted.

Philly Steak Sandwiches

I used to really enjoy the original, but it was simply too heavy and cheesy for my body to tolerate. This one is a light and tasty alternative that even your meat eating friends will enjoy.

2 medium green peppers, julienned
1 small onion, sliced
1 Tablespoon oil
1 package Lightlife Smart Strips ® Steak
Salt and pepper to taste
¼ cup vegan butter or margarine, softened
1 cup of shredded Vegan Cheddar
4 long rolls, split and toasted

In a skillet, cook green peppers and onion in oil until vegetables are tender.

Add steak strips and salt and pepper, and cook until warm, 3-5 minutes.

Place cheese on the bottom of each roll, then add steak mixture on top.

Sourdough Special

1 medium onion, sliced
1 cup sliced fresh mushrooms
1 cup julienned green pepper
1 cup julienned sweet red pepper
2 Tablespoons vegetable oil
12 slices sourdough bread
1 package of hickory smoked Tofurky®
1 package of Lightlife or other vegan Ham
6 Lightlife or other vegan bacon strips, cooked
6 slices of vegan American cheese

In a large skillet, cook the onion, mushrooms, and peppers in oil until tender.

Layer six slices of bread with ham, turkey, bacon, vegetables and cheese; top with remaining bread.

Coat pan with non-stick spray or butter and grill each sandwich over medium heat for 2-3 minutes on each side or until heated through.

Strawberry Banana Almond Toasts (GF)

Makes a quick and yummy breakfast or sweet treat that is way better than those plates of fruity pancakes so many restaurants are serving these days.

    2 Tablespoons almond or other nut butter
    1 Tablespoon strawberry jam
    ½ banana, sliced
    4 fresh strawberries, sliced
    2 slices bread of choice

Spread almond/nut butter over one side of one slice of bread.

Arrange strawberries and bananas over almond butter. Spread jam over one side of remaining slice of bread.

Place over fruit to make a sandwich.

Serve cold, or wrap in aluminum, and bake in the oven or toaster oven 3-5 minutes until warm.

Sausage and Peppers Parmesan

A remake of one of my favorite Italian subs.

1 package of Lightlife Gimme Lean® Sausage
1 medium onion, chopped
1 (14 ounce) jar pizza sauce
1 (14 ounce) can of diced tomatoes, drained
4 long rolls or other bread of choice
1 ½ cups shredded vegan Mozzarella cheese
Vegan Parmesan topping

In a skillet over medium heat, cook peppers and onions until soft and the onion begins to brown.

Stir in sauce and cook and stir for 5 minutes. Crumble sausage and stir into sauce.

Turn down heat to low and cover, simmering for 10 minutes, stirring occasionally. Stir in tomatoes and cook another 5 minutes.

Place bread or buns, cut side up, on baking sheets. Broil 4 inches from the heat until lightly toasted.

Spread about 3 Tablespoons sausage mixture over each bun half or bread slice. Sprinkle with cheeses. Broil for 2-3 minutes or until cheese is melted.

Sloppy Joes

You can always use your favorite canned Sloppy Joe sauce, but now that you see how easy it is, you may prefer to make your own from now on.

1 package of Gimme Lean® Beef
½ cup ketchup
2 Tablespoons water
1 Tablespoon brown sugar or any sweetener of choice
1 teaspoon vegan Worcestershire sauce
1 teaspoon mustard
¼ teaspoon garlic powder
¼ teaspoon onion powder
¼ teaspoon salt
Hamburger buns, split

In a saucepan, stir together ketchup, water, brown sugar/sweetener, Worcestershire sauce, mustard, garlic powder, onion powder and salt. Bring to a boil for about one minute.

Reduce heat and add beef, making sure to break into small pieces. Cover and simmer for 20-30 minutes on very low heat, to allow beef to absorb sauce. Stir regularly, as the beef product has a tendency to stick. Serve on buns.

Meatball Parmesan

Serve with our Mozzarella sticks found in our sides section, and you're like me, you will never miss being vegan again.

1 package of Gimme Lean® Beef
½ cup bread crumbs
2 teaspoons of oregano
1 clove of garlic, minced
2 Tablespoons chopped fresh parsley
2 Tablespoons vegan Parmesan cheese
1 loaf of Italian bread or other bread of choice
½ teaspoon garlic powder
2 (14 ounce) jars spaghetti sauce
1 cup shredded vegan Mozzarella cheese

Preheat the oven to 350°F.

In a medium bowl, gently mix by hand the beef, bread crumbs, oregano, garlic, parsley, and Parmesan cheese. Shape into 12 meatballs, and place in a baking dish. Cover with one of the jars of sauce.

Bake for 15 minutes.

Meanwhile, cut the bread in half lengthwise, and remove some of the bread from the inside to make a well for the meatballs. Slip the baguette into the oven during the last 5 minutes of the meatball's time, or until lightly toasted.

While the bread toasts, warm the remaining jar of spaghetti sauce in a saucepan over medium heat. When the meatballs are done, use a slotted spoon to transfer them to the extra sauce. Spoon onto the baguette and top with shredded Mozzarella. Return to the oven for 2 to 3 minutes to melt the cheese. Cool slightly, then cut into servings.

Roasted Eggplant (GF)

Eggplant, much like Portabellas, have a nice, chewy texture that can mimic beef. Roasting also intensifies the flavor and nutrients.

1 small eggplant, halved and sliced
1 Tablespoon oil
2 cloves of garlic, minced
2 (6 inch) sandwich rolls or other bread of choice
1 small tomato, sliced
½ cup vegan Mozzarella cheese
¼ cup chopped fresh basil leaves

Preheat your oven's broiler. Brush eggplant slices with oil, and place them on a baking sheet or broiling pan.

Place the pan about 6 inches from the heat source. Cook under the broiler for 10 minutes, or until brown and toasted.

Split the rolls lengthwise, and toast. Fill the rolls with eggplant slices, tomato, cheese, and basil leaves.

Reuben

An authentic Reuben uses Thousand Island dressing. I prefer mine without dressing these days, but am offering the recipe here for you to decide.

Gluten-Free idea: Substitute grilled tempeh for the turkey slices.

8 slices rye or our Not Rye bread
Vegan Thousand Island dressing, optional (see recipe below)
1 (16 ounce) can sauerkraut, drained
8 slices vegan cheese, any variety
1 package of peppercorn flavor Tofurky® slices
¼ cup vegan margarine, softened

Thousand Island Dressing

2 Tablespoons vegan sour cream
1 Tablespoon of vegan mayonnaise
2 Tablespoons of relish
1 Tablespoon of ketchup

Spread each slice of bread with Thousand Island dressing (if using).

Top 4 of the bread slices with sauerkraut, cheese and turkey. Place remaining bread slices on sandwich. Spread margarine on the outsides of each sandwich.

Heat a large skillet over medium high heat. Grill until browned, then turn and grill until heated through, and cheese is melted.

Tofu Spread (GF)

1 pound firm tofu, frozen, defrosted, and drained
1 stalk celery, chopped
1 green onion, chopped
½ cup vegan mayonnaise
2 Tablespoons wheat-free tamari or soy sauce
1 Tablespoon lemon juice

Drain tofu and freeze overnight.

Thaw, and squeeze out any moisture by hand, then wrap in paper towels, placing a heavy weight on it for at least 30 minutes.

Remove towels and mash with a fork.

Add celery and green onion to the tofu. Stir in mayonnaise, soy sauce/tamari and lemon juice until well blended.

Refrigerate at least 2 hours before serving.

Hummus Pita (GF)

1 can garbanzo beans, rinsed and drained
¼ cup Tahini (sesame butter)
1 clove garlic, minced
1 teaspoon salt
1 pinch paprika
1 teaspoon olive oil
1 Tablespoon water
2 Tablespoons fresh lemon juice
A pinch salt
½ cucumber, thinly sliced
1 large tomato, sliced
1 small red onion, thinly sliced
4 pitas

Place the garbanzo beans, tahini, garlic, salt, and paprika into a blender.

Add oil, water, lemon juice, and any other desired spices. Puree until smooth, and set aside.

Assemble on pitas with lettuce, tomatoes, cucumber, and red onion.

Pizza Subs (GF)

1(14 oz) jar of pizza sauce
1 loaf of Italian bread or other bread of choice
½ cup sliced mushrooms
½ cup sliced black olives
1 large green pepper, thinly sliced
½ cup diced onions
1 cup shredded vegan Mozzarella cheese
Oregano, basil, and vegan Parmesan cheese, to taste

Preheat oven to 350°F.

Cut loaf in half and spread pizza sauce on both sides, or add sauce to each slice of bread.

Divide toppings equally, adding cheese last. If desired, add oregano, basil, and vegan Parmesan on top.

Bake for 15 minutes or until cheese is bubbly. Serve hot.

Variations: You can add vegan pepperoni, beef, chicken, or other veggies and cheese options.

Un-Tuna (GF)

I like the versatility of this recipe. The tuna alone can be used in any recipe that calls for tuna, or mixed with tartar (or regular vegan mayo) it is a great sandwich or salad spread.

Tuna

1 pound of firm tofu, drained and mashed
½ teaspoon kelp powder (this really provides the tuna flavor)
¼ teaspoon garlic powder
¼ teaspoon paprika
¼ teaspoon onion powder
¼ cup finely minced celery
Salt and pepper to taste

Tartar Sauce

½ cup vegan mayonnaise
¼ cup dill pickle relish
1 Tablespoon fresh lemon juice

Prepare tartar sauce and set aside.

To make tuna, mix all ingredients and stir in tartar sauce to desired consistency. Refrigerate. Serve cold or as tuna melts.

Vegan Club

This is a good recipe for parties. I like to make these and their traditional counterpart, side by side. It shows my meat eating friends that I am by no means suffering!

2 slices bread, any variety
2 teaspoons yellow mustard
2 slices LightLife® Canadian Bacon slices
2 slices Tofurky® turkey, any flavor
2 slices Lightlife® Bacon
1 slice vegan cheese, any variety
Vegan butter or margarine, for coating bread

Spread bread with butter. Place both buttered sides face down in a skillet over medium heat. Spread mustard on the sides facing up, then alternate ham, cheese, turkey, and bacon slices on top of one slice.

Check the plain slice of bread. When the bottom side is browned, assemble sandwich and serve hot.

Walnut and Mushroom Spread

I first made this for my good pal, Lucy one Thanksgiving, who has multiple food allergies. Initially created as a dip for veggies and crackers, she immediately turned it into a sandwich on gluten-free bread and called it dinner. I learned later she had the right idea.

1 cup walnuts
½ cup minced shallots
½ cup vegan butter
¼ pound shiitake mushrooms, chopped
¼ pound crimini mushrooms, chopped
¼ pound portobella mushrooms, chopped
1 Tablespoon minced garlic
¼ cup chopped fresh Italian parsley
½ teaspoon salt
½ teaspoon white pepper
2 Tablespoons extra-virgin olive oil *or* walnut oil

Preheat oven to 350°F. Spread walnuts in a single layer on a cookie sheet. Toast for 10 minutes, or until lightly browned.

In a large frying pan, cook shallots in butter over medium heat until translucent. Add chopped mushrooms, garlic, parsley, salt, and pepper. Cook, stirring often, until most of the liquid has evaporated.

Blend walnuts and oil in a blender or food processor until mixture forms a thick paste. Spoon in the cooked mushroom mixture, and process to desired texture.

For best flavor, refrigerate for a few hours or overnight before serving.

Veggie Spread (GF)

I consider this one of my "earthy" meals that I often bring to vegan potlucks and gatherings. While you can use any type of bread, I prefer it with pitas or wrappers.

1 cup sunflower seeds
½ cup whole wheat or gluten-free flour
½ cup nutritional yeast
½ teaspoon salt
½ cup oil
2 Tablespoons lemon juice
1 potato, peeled and chopped
1 large carrot, peeled and sliced
1 onion, chopped
1 stalk celery, chopped
1 clove garlic, peeled
1½ cups water
½ teaspoon oregano
½ teaspoon black pepper
Bread, lettuce, tomato, sprouts, avocado, etc., for sandwiches

Preheat oven to 350°F. Lightly grease an 8x8 inch baking dish.

In a food processor, blend sunflower seeds with all other ingredients. Process the mixture until almost smooth.

Transfer mixture to the baking dish. Bake 1 hour, or until bubbly and lightly browned. Serve warm or cold as sandwiches.

Lentil Spread

Lentils are high in iron and protein and luckily, have a nice hearty flavor that many adore.

1 cup dry lentils
2 cups vegetable broth
2 teaspoons extra virgin olive oil
½ cup salsa
Salt and pepper to taste

Boil lentils in broth in a covered pan until the lentils are soft and all the broth has been absorbed, about 30 minutes. If needed, add more broth until the lentils are done.

Remove from heat, and let cool.

Place lentils in a food processor. Pour in oil, and pulse until almost smooth. Season with salt and pepper to taste, and add additional oil if desired. Pulse to preferred thickness and consistency.

Stir in ½ cup salsa. Refrigerate at least one hour before serving.

White Bean and Green Sammy (GF)

2 (15 ounce) cans cannellini beans, rinsed and drained
1/3 cup spinach or any other leafy green
1clove of garlic, minced
¼ cup olive oil
1 lemon, juiced
Salt and pepper to taste
Naan or other flatbread, regular or gluten-free

Sandwich Makings

Salad or other leafy greens
Green olives, sliced
Salsa

In a food processor, combine the cannellini beans, spinach/greens, garlic, olive oil and lemon juice. Process until smooth, or to your desired consistency. Taste, and season with salt and pepper.

Refrigerate at least one hour.

To serve, spread white beans over flatbread, top with salsa and any other sandwich makings. Wrap in foil, and warm in a skillet, 2-3 minutes, turn with tongs, and continue to warm 2-3 more minutes. Open carefully.

Spicy Mexican Wraps (GF)

1 (15 ounce) can refried beans
1 (15 ounce) can black beans, rinsed and drained
¾ cup vegan sour cream
1 cup salsa
1 (4 ounce) can diced jalapeno peppers
1 ½ cups shredded vegan cheese
¼ cup sliced black olives
½ cup guacamole (optional)
½ cup cooked white or brown rice
Wrappers, regular or gluten-free

Preheat an oven to 375°F.

Combine refried beans and black beans in the bottom of baking dish.

Top with sour cream, salsa, jalapenos, olives, and cheese.

Cover dish, and bake for 15 minutes. Uncover, and bake until hot and bubbly, about 15 additional minutes.

When done, remove from oven. Assemble wraps by first filling with rice, then guacamole if using, then the bean filling. Add optional additional cheese, salsa, and sour cream.

Edamame Spread (GF)

Edamame are soybeans that are easily found in most freezer sections of most grocery stores.

2 cloves garlic
2 Tablespoons olive oil
1 teaspoon hot pepper sauce, or to taste
½ teaspoon cumin
1 cup frozen shelled edamame, thawed
1 Tablespoon water, as needed
Salt and pepper to taste
½ cup edamame, to stir into finished product
Bread of choice

Place the garlic cloves, olive oil, hot sauce, and cumin into a blender.

Puree until smooth, then add the edamame, and continue to puree until smooth. Add water as needed to achieve your desired consistency.

Stir in ½ cup edamame for added texture.

Season to taste with salt and pepper.

Falafel (GF)

When I first learned that these "Middle Eastern Meatballs" as I first introduced to them were vegan, I used them in all sorts of creative ways. With the right bread crumbs, they can be gluten-free, too.

1 (15 ounce) can chickpeas (garbanzo beans), drained
1 onion, chopped
½ cup fresh parsley
1 clove of garlic, chopped
¼ cup mashed tofu
1 teaspoon ground coriander
1 teaspoon salt
1 dash pepper
1 teaspoon lemon juice
1 teaspoon baking powder
1 Tablespoon olive oil
1 cup dry bread crumbs, regular or gluten-free
Oil for frying
Salt and pepper to taste
Pitas, hummus, and veggies of choice

In a large bowl mash chickpeas by hand with a fork. In a blender, process onion, parsley and garlic until smooth. Stir into mashed chickpeas.

In a small bowl combine tofu, coriander, salt, pepper, lemon juice, and baking powder. Stir into chickpea mixture along with olive oil. Slowly add bread crumbs until mixture is not sticky but will hold together; You may need to add more or less bread crumbs than the recipe calls for, as needed. Form 8 balls and then flatten into patties.

Heat 1 inch of oil in a large skillet over medium-high heat. Fry patties in hot oil until brown on both sides. Assemble pitas by first adding some hummus, lettuce, tomato, and any other sandwich makings, then add the falafel.

Burgers

Burgers are the perfect portable meal that can be made out of so many things other than meat. While veggie-based patties are readily available, many have eggs and dairy.

Carrot Burgers (GF)

These make for an interesting side dish or appetizer, and also make for a light and healthy burger meal with baked fries.

1 ½ cups diced carrots
2 cups crushed cornflakes, regular or gluten-free
½ cup mashed tofu
¼ cup finely chopped celery
1 Tablespoon finely chopped onion
½ teaspoon salt
1 teaspoon agave nectar or other sweetener of choice
A pinch of black pepper
2 Tablespoons vegetable oil
6 Buns/bread of choice

Place carrots in a saucepan with a small amount of water. Bring to a boil; reduce heat. Cover and cook for 5 minutes or until tender; drain.

In a bowl, combine carrots, cornflakes, tofu, celery, onion, salt, sugar and pepper; mix well. Form into six patties.

Heat oil in a skillet over medium heat; cook patties for 3 minutes on each side or until browned. Serve with optional cheese.

Grain Burgers

I created this recipe totally by accident. I dropped some rice into polenta, scooped it out in an attempt to salvage the polenta, and realized I came up with a very tasty dish.

2 Tablespoons vegan butter, divided
1 cup cooked rice, any variety
1 clove garlic, chopped
1 teaspoon of oregano
5 cups water, divided
2 cups dry polenta
3/4 cup vegan Cheddar cheese
Salt and pepper to taste

Melt 1 Tablespoon of the butter in a large pot set over medium heat.

Add the rice and, garlic, and oregano; cook and stir until the rice is coated.

Pour in 2 cups of the water and bring to a boil. Cover, reduce heat to low and simmer for 10 minutes.

Increase heat to medium and stir in the polenta. Gradually stir in the remaining water as the polenta absorbs it. When all of the water is absorbed, mix in the remaining butter and cheese. Reduce heat to low and simmer, stirring frequently for about 20 minutes.

Butter a large baking dish and pour the mixture into it. Spread into an even layer if necessary and set aside to cool and become firm.

When the mixture cools, tap it out onto a cutting board and cut into squares. Fry patties until golden on each side. Serve with your favorite toppings.

Lentil Burgers (GF)

These are really tasty with fried onions.

1 cup dry brown lentils
2 ½ cups vegetable stock
¼ cup unflavored milk product
1 cup cooked brown or white rice
½ cup tofu, mashed
½ cup chopped walnuts
1 cup seasoned bread crumbs, regular or gluten-free
2 Tablespoons oil
Salt and pepper, to taste
Buns, lettuce, tomato, pickles, and other burger makings

Place lentils and stock in a saucepan, and bring to a boil. Cover, reduce heat to low, and simmer until tender, about 30 minutes. Drain.

In a large bowl, mix together the cooked lentils, milk, rice, tofu, walnuts, and salt and pepper. Mix well using your hands, as the mixture will be very thick. Let stand for 30 minutes, or refrigerate overnight.

Heat oil in a large skillet over medium heat. Use an ice cream scoop to portion out balls of the lentil mixture. Drop the scoops into bread crumbs, and coat while flattening into patties. Fry burgers about 5 minutes or until brown, then turn and repeat. Serve as desired.

Chickpea Burgers (GF)

1 can garbanzo beans, drained and mashed
1 ½ cups cooked brown rice
½ cup bread crumbs, regular or gluten-free
1 pound of firm tofu
¼ cup barbeque sauce
Salt and pepper to taste
½ teaspoon garlic powder
2 teaspoons vegetable oil
½ teaspoon each oregano and basil

In a large bowl, stir together the mashed garbanzo beans and spices. Mix in the rice and bread crumbs. The mixture should seem a little dry.

In a separate bowl, mash the tofu with your hands, trying to squeeze out as much of the water as possible. Pour the barbeque sauce over the tofu, and stir to coat.

Stir the tofu into the garbanzo bean mixture until well blended.

Heat the oil in a large skillet over medium-high heat. Form patties and fry for about 5 minutes per side. Serve with your favorite toppings and sides.

Black Bean Burgers (GF)

These are my favorite bean burgers. I like to top them with salsa and vegan Cheddar.

½ cup uncooked brown rice
1 cup water
2 (16 ounce) cans black beans, rinsed and drained
1 green bell pepper, halved and seeded
1 onion, quartered
½ cup sliced mushrooms
2 cloves garlic, peeled
¾ cup vegan Cheddar cheese
½ cup mashed tofu
1 Tablespoon chili powder
1 teaspoon ground cumin
1 teaspoon hot sauce
½ cup bread crumbs, or as needed

Bring the brown rice and water to a boil in a saucepan over high heat. Reduce the heat to medium-low, cover, and simmer until the rice is tender, and the liquid has been absorbed, 45 to 50 minutes.

Mash black beans in a large bowl with a fork until thick and pasty; set aside. Place the bell pepper, onion, mushrooms, and garlic in the bowl of a food processor, and chop finely. Stir the bell pepper mixture into the mashed black beans. Place the brown rice and cheese in the food processor, and process until combined. Stir the mixture into the black beans.

Whisk together the tofu, chili powder, cumin, and hot sauce. Stir the tofu into the black bean mixture. Stir in the bread crumbs, adding additional bread crumbs as needed until the mixture is sticky and holds together. Divide into 6 large patties.

Fry over medium heat, 5-7 minutes on each side, until browned.

Portabella Burgers

These work well on the grill for BBQ season but you can always cook them indoors on the stove.

4 Portobella mushroom caps
¼ cup balsamic vinegar
2 Tablespoons oil
1 teaspoon dried basil
1 teaspoon dried oregano
1 Tablespoon minced garlic
Salt and pepper to taste
4 slices of any flavor vegan cheese

Place the mushroom caps, smooth side up, in a shallow dish. In a small bowl, whisk together vinegar, oil, basil, oregano, garlic, salt, and pepper. Pour over the mushrooms. Let stand at room temperature for 1 hour, turning twice.

Preheat grill for medium-high heat or heat oil in a large skillet.

If grilling, brush grate with oil. Place mushrooms on the grill, reserving marinade for basting.

Whether grilling for frying, cook for 5 to 8 minutes on each side, or until tender. Brush with marinade frequently. Top with cheese during the last 2 minutes of cooking.

Chili Burgers (GF)

Why make chili when you can make it into a burger?

1 carrot, sliced
1 (15 ounce) can kidney beans
½ cup chopped green pepper
½ cup chopped onion
2 cups salsa
1 cup bread crumbs, regular or gluten-free
½ cup flour, regular or gluten-free
Salt and pepper to taste
A pinch chili powder

Place carrots in a bowl, and cover with water. Microwave for 2 minutes, or until soft. Drain.

Mash beans and carrots together in a large bowl. Mix in green pepper, onions, salsa, bread crumbs, and flour. Season with salt, pepper, and chili powder.

Add flour to create a firmer mixture, or more salsa if the mixture is too stiff.

Shape into 8 patties, and place on a greased baking sheet.

Heat a large skillet over medium-high heat, and coat with cooking spray. Fry the patties for about 8 minutes on each side, or until browned.

Veggie Patties (GF)

2 teaspoons of oil
1 small onion, grated
1 clove of minced garlic
2 carrots, shredded
1 yellow squash, shredded
1 small zucchini, shredded
1 ½ cups rolled oats, regular or gluten-free
¼ cup shredded vegan Cheddar cheese
½ cup tofu, mashed
1 Tablespoon soy sauce or wheat-free tamari
1 ½ cups all-purpose flour, regular or gluten-free

Heat the oil in a skillet over low heat, and cook the onion and garlic for about 5 minutes, until tender. Mix in the carrots, squash, and zucchini. Continue to cook for another 2 minutes.

Remove pan from heat, and mix in oats, cheese, and tofu. Stir in soy sauce/tamari, and transfer the mixture to a bowl. Refrigerate 1 hour.

Place the flour on a large plate. Form the vegetable mixture into 8 patties of equal size. Drop each patty into the flour, lightly coating both sides.

Oil a large skillet and pan fry patties, 5-7 minutes over medium heat on each side.

Zucchini Burgers

This is a wonderful recipe when your garden overflows with zucchini. Be creative and add in other grated vegetables you have an overabundance of.

2 cups grated zucchini
½ cup tofu, mashed
¼ cup chopped onion
½ cup all-purpose flour, regular or gluten-free
½ cup vegan Parmesan cheese
½ cup shredded vegan Mozzarella cheese
Salt and pepper to taste
2 Tablespoons oil

In a medium bowl, combine the zucchini, tofu, onion, flour, cheeses, and salt and pepper. Stir well enough to distribute ingredients evenly.

Heat a small amount of oil in a skillet over medium-high heat. Drop zucchini mixture by heaping Tablespoonfuls, and cook for a few minutes on each side until golden.

Tofu Patties

Egg Replacer for two eggs, prepared according to package
2 (16 ounce) packages firm tofu
2 stalks celery, minced
1 small onion, minced
1 Tablespoon chili powder
1 Tablespoon ground cumin
1 Tablespoon minced garlic
2 cups rolled oats, regular or gluten-free
1 Tablespoon oil

Prepare egg replacer in a mixing bowl. Mix in the tofu, celery, onion, chili powder, cumin, garlic, and oats with your hands until the tofu has broken into fine pieces, and the mixture is evenly blended. Form into 8 patties.

Heat the oil in a large, nonstick skillet over medium heat. Cook the patties until crispy and golden brown on each side, about 5 minutes per side.

Quinoa Burgers

Quinoa is an ancient South American grain that is gluten-free and higher in protein than any other grain. It cooks quickly and is very versatile.

1 ½ cups cooked quinoa
½ cup hummus
1 Tablespoon tomato paste
2 Tablespoons ground flaxseed meal
1 Tablespoon wheat-free tamari
½ teaspoon ground cumin
½ teaspoon paprika
¼ cup tapioca starch
Salt and pepper to taste

Heat a non-stick frying pan on med. low

Blend all ingredients in a bowl or food processor.

Press into 8 patties.

Fry in a little oil on medium heat, 5 - 10 minutes each side, until browned and firm.

Nut Burgers

Long ago, this was the traditional vegetarian burger. They are quite easy to make and are quite the crowd pleaser.

½ cup finely chopped walnuts
½ cup unsalted sunflower seeds
1 cup canned chickpeas, drained
¼ cup diced red onion
1 portion of Egg replacer, prepared according to package
1 Tablespoon chopped fresh parsley
¼ teaspoon black pepper
1 teaspoon of salt
2 Tablespoons oil
2 slices vegan Cheddar cheese
1 pita bread round

Place walnuts and sunflower seeds in a dry skillet over medium heat. Cook, stirring occasionally until lightly toasted, about 5 minutes.

In a medium bowl, mash garbanzo beans. Stir in the onion, egg replacer, parsley, and nuts. Season with salt and pepper, and mix well.

Heat oil in a skillet over medium heat. Divide the bean mixture into 2 patties, and fry in the hot oil for about 3 minutes on each side, or until well browned and heated through. Place a slice of cheese over each patty, and remove from heat.

Serve on buns or pita with your choice of toppings.

Sides

I gathered some recipes from some of my previous books, as well as some new ones, that make great sides to your sandwiches and burgers. Be creative!

Baked Potato Skins (GF)

I am such a fan of potatoes that when I was trying to lose weight ages ago, I would not consider a high-protein diet because I would have to give up potatoes and not because I would have to eat all that meat, which I really do not care for in the least.

4 large baking potatoes, baked
3 Tablespoons vegetable oil
1 Tablespoon vegan Parmesan cheese
½ teaspoon salt
¼ teaspoon garlic powder
¼ teaspoon paprika
1 ½ cups shredded vegan Cheddar cheese
½ cup vegan sour cream
2 green onions, sliced
½ cup broccoli florets, chopped small

Preheat oven to 475°F.

Cut potatoes in half lengthwise; scoop out pulp, leaving a 1/4-inch shell (save pulp for another use).

Place potatoes skins on a greased baking sheet.

Combine oil, Parmesan cheese, broccoli, salt, garlic powder, and paprika; brush over both sides of skins.

Bake for 7 minutes; turn. Continue to bake until crisp, about 7 minutes more. Sprinkle Cheddar cheese inside skins. Bake 2 minutes longer or until the cheese is melted. Top with sour cream and onions. Serve immediately.

Mozzarella Sticks (GF)

1 8oz block of vegan Mozzarella (I use Follow Your Heart)
Oil for frying

Wet Ingredients

½ cup gluten-free all-purpose flour
½ cup water
1 Tablespoon cornmeal
1 Tablespoon cornstarch
salt, oregano, pepper, garlic powder, and other desired spices
to taste

Dry Ingredients

1 cup gluten-free breadcrumbs
½ teaspoon salt
½ teaspoon parsley flakes
½ teaspoon black pepper
½ teaspoon garlic powder
¼ teaspoon onion powder
¼ teaspoon oregano
¼ teaspoon basil

Combine ingredients for wet mix. The consistency should be like pancake batter, so adjust accordingly if needed. In another bowl, stir together breadcrumbs and remaining spices. Remove vegan cheese from refrigerator and slice into ½" strips.

Lightly coat each stick with flour. Dredge each stick in the wet mix, then toss in bread crumbs until fully coated. Place sticks on a cookie sheet in a single layer, not touching one another, and freeze for at least one hour.

Heat up your deep fryer, or if you don't have one, pour an inch of (safflower or peanut have the highest heat tolerance) oil into the bottom of a deep skillet or deep fryer and heat.

Carefully dip the end of a stick into the oil to check for readiness; if the oil sizzles continually, it's ready. If not, let it heat up some more.

Once it's up to temperature, fry sticks in small batches so they do not crowd the pan and reduce the oil's heat too much. Fry about 1 minute per side, or until they're golden brown and you can see a little cheese oozing through the breadcrumbs. Serve with marinara sauce for dipping.

Stuffed Tomatoes (GF)

A great light meal, side, or yummy appetizer.

4 large firm tomatoes
2 Tablespoons of olive oil
½ cup red onion, diced small
2 cups cooked rice, white or brown
¼ teaspoon of oregano
Salt and pepper to taste

Preheat oven to 350°F.

Cut ½ inch off the top of each of tomato. Use a small knife or a melon baller to gently scoop out the insides of the tomatoes, being careful not to cut through the bottoms.

Sauté the onions for a few minutes in olive oil, until soft.

In a large bowl, combine the remaining ingredients. Using a small spoon, scoop the rice mixture and stuff each tomato. Gently pack in the rice, so the whole tomato is full.

Lightly brush the tomatoes with a bit olive oil and place in a baking dish. Bake for 25 minutes, or until the tomatoes are soft and begin to shrivel. Do not over bake.

Kale Chips (GF)

I love kale any way I can get it, but this recipe is equally good with any leafy greens or a mix.

1 bunch kale
1 Tablespoon oil
1 teaspoon seasoned salt

Preheat an oven to 350°. Line a cookie sheet with parchment paper.

Carefully remove the leaves from the thick stems and tear into bite size pieces. Wash and thoroughly dry kale. Drizzle kale with oil and sprinkle with season salt.

Bake until the edges brown but are not burnt, about 10 to 15 minutes.

Onion Rings (GF)*

Just a few of these really hit the spot.

1 quart oil for frying
1 cup all-purpose flour, regular or gluten-free
1 cup beer* (see note)
1 pinch each salt black pepper
4 onions, peeled and sliced into rings

In a large, deep skillet, heat oil to 365°F.

In a medium bowl, combine flour, beer*, salt, and pepper. Mix until smooth.

Dredge onion slices in the batter, until evenly coated.

Deep fry in the hot oil in small batches until golden brown. Watch carefully as they can burn quite quickly. Drain on paper towels.

* Gluten-free beer is being manufactured, but if you cannot find it, feel free to use water.

Sweet Potato Chips (GF)

You can also make these sweet by omitting the cayenne and adding cinnamon instead.

2 Tablespoons oil
2 Tablespoons maple syrup, regular or sugar-free
¼ teaspoon cayenne pepper, optional
3 large sweet potatoes, peeled and cut into ¼ -inch slices
Salt and pepper to taste

Preheat oven to 450°F. Line a baking sheet with aluminum foil.

Stir together the oil, maple syrup, and cayenne pepper in a small bowl.

Brush the sweet potato slices with the maple mixture and place onto the baking sheet. Sprinkle with salt and pepper to taste.

Bake for 8 minutes, then turn and brush with remaining maple mixture. Continue baking until tender in the middle, and crispy on the edges, about 7 minutes more.

Baked French Fries (GF)
Just as yummy, and much lower in fat, than traditional fries.

3 russet potatoes, sliced into ¼ inch strips
Non-stick cooking spray
1 teaspoon dried oregano, optional
¼ cup vegan Parmesan cheese
Salt and pepper to taste

Preheat oven to 400°F. Lightly grease a medium baking sheet with non-stick cooking spray.

Arrange potato strips in a single layer on baking sheet, skin sides down.

Spray lightly with cooking spray, and sprinkle with any spices you may be using, Parmesan cheese, salt and pepper.

Bake for 25 minutes, or until golden brown.

Broccoli Salad

You can vary this recipe by using equally parts of broccoli and cauliflower.

2 heads fresh broccoli
1 red onion
¾ cup raisins
¾ cup sliced almonds or other nuts
1 cup vegan mayonnaise
½ cup granulated sweetener of choice
2 Tablespoons white wine vinegar

Cut the broccoli into bite-size pieces and cut the onion into thin bite-size slices. Combine with the raisins and nuts, and mix well.

To prepare the dressing, mix the mayonnaise, sweetener and vinegar together until smooth. Stir into the salad, let chill and serve.

Cabbage Salad (GF)

A fresher, healthier option to cole slaw.

1 cup olive oil
2 cups red wine vinegar
1 Tablespoon sweetener of choice
1 teaspoon salt
¼ teaspoon ground black pepper
¼ teaspoon onion powder
1 head red cabbage, cored and thickly shredded
1 head of green cabbage, cored and thickly shredded

In a bowl, mix the oil, vinegar, sweetener, salt, pepper, and onion powder.

Place the cabbage in a large bowl. Pour dressing over cabbage, and toss to coat.

Cover, and refrigerate 8 hours, or overnight, stirring occasionally.

Drain before serving.

Red Potato Salad

I prefer using oil and vinegar to vegan mayonnaise in this recipe, as the veggie bacon really marinates and lends it flavor over better.

  2 pounds of small red potatoes
  1 package of Lightlife or other vegan bacon
  1 onion, finely chopped
  1 stalk celery, finely chopped
  1 cup olive oil
  2 cups balsamic vinegar
  Salt and pepper to taste

Bring a large pot of salted water to a boil. Add potatoes and cook until tender but still firm, about 15 minutes. Drain and set in the refrigerator to cool.

Place bacon in a large skillet. Coat pan with oil or non-stick spray. Cook over medium heat until evenly brown. Crumble and set aside.

Chop the cooled potatoes, leaving skin on. Add to a large bowl, along with the bacon, onion and celery.

Add oil and vinegar, salt and pepper to taste. Chill for at least an hour before serving.

Corn Tortilla Chips

These are easier to make than you think. Feel free to try using other tortillas other than corn and change up the spices. I really like gluten-free tortillas with cinnamon and sweetener.

1 quart oil for frying
1 (12 ounce) package corn tortillas, cut into 6 wedges each
Salt to taste

Heat oil in a large, heavy saucepan to 375°F.

In small batches, fry the corn tortilla wedges until crisp.

Remove from heat and drain on paper towels.

Salt to taste while warm.

Carrot Raisin Salad

I have had equal success using shredded zucchini and yellow squash. For a colorful variation, use a blend of all three.

½ cup vegan sour cream
½ cup vegan mayonnaise
1 Tablespoon lemon juice
½ teaspoon salt
1 Tablespoon sweetener of choice
4 cups shredded carrot
1 cup raisins

In a large bowl, whisk together the sour cream, mayonnaise, lemon juice, salt and sweetener.

Add carrots and raisins and stir until coated.

Spicy Homemade Pickles

Who knew making pickles was this easy? You can also pickle peppers, beets, and okra while you're at it.

12 (3 to 4 inch) long pickling cucumbers
2 cups water
1 ¾ cups white vinegar
1 ½ cups chopped fresh dill weed
½ cup granulated sweetener
2 cloves garlic, chopped
1 ½ Tablespoons coarse salt
1 Tablespoon pickling spice
1 ½ teaspoons dill seed
½ teaspoon red pepper flakes, or to taste

In a large bowl, combine the cucumbers, water, vinegar, chopped dill, sweetener/sugar, garlic, salt, pickling spice, dill seed, and red pepper flakes. Stir, and let stand at room temperature for 2 hours, until the sweetener and salt dissolve.

Remove the cucumbers to three 1 ½ pint wide mouth jars, placing 4 cucumbers into each jar.

Ladle in the liquid from the bowl to cover. Seal with lids. Refrigerate for 10 days before eating.

Store in the refrigerator for one month.

Veggie Pasta Salad (GF)

You can make a pasta salad out of any type of pasta and any veggies on hand. However, this is my favorite combination.

1 (16 ounce) package spiral pasta, regular or gluten-free
1 cup broccoli florets
1 cup cauliflower florets
1 cup chopped carrots
½ cup diced zucchini
1 cup cherry tomatoes
1/4 cup chopped onion
1 (6.5 ounce) jar marinated artichoke hearts, drained and halved
1 (8 ounce) bottle Italian salad dressing, or your own favorite

Cook pasta according to package directions; drain and rinse in cold water.

Place in a large bowl; add remaining ingredients and toss to coat.

Cover and refrigerate for 2 hours or overnight.

Breads

Bread is perhaps my favorite food of all and was my first missed when I had to give up refined white flour and most gluten products.

These days, gluten-free breads are popping up in almost every grocery store. However, for those of you who cannot find what you need, or prefer to make your own, I have included some of my favorite recipes from my book, *"The Virtuous Vegan"*.

Focaccia

A thick, seasoned bread that doubles as a pan pizza crust and a wonderful bread for many of my spreads and sandwiches.

Whisk together:

1 cup sorghum flour
1 cup tapioca starch
½ cup potato flour
2 teaspoons xanthan gum
1 ¼ teaspoons sea salt
1 teaspoon dried minced onion
½ teaspoon garlic powder
2 teaspoons dried oregano
2 teaspoons dried basil

Prepare in a glass bowl or measuring cup

Add 1 Tablespoon active dry yeast:
1 ¼ cups water at 110°F
A pinch of granulated sweetener

When the yeast is ready, pour the mixture into the dry ingredients and add:

4 Tablespoons extra virgin olive oil
1 Tablespoon agave nectar
½ teaspoon o lemon juice
Egg replacer for 1 egg prepared according to box instructions

Stir to combine. The dough should be sticky and resemble muffin batter, not dough. Dust a round pan with cornmeal and add focaccia. Wet your hand and shape into a rounded loaf. Place the pan into the warm oven and allow it to rise for 20 minutes. Preheat oven to 375°F and bake 25 minutes or until golden.

Chapati

Chapatis are thin, flat breads that are eaten much like what we know in the US as wraps. Great for many of our spreads.

1 cup amaranth flour
½ cup millet flour
½ cup sorghum flour
½ cup tapioca starch
2 teaspoons xanthan gum
1 teaspoon salt
1 teaspoon baking powder

Add in:
3 Tablespoons olive oil
1 Tablespoon agave nectar
Egg replacer for 2 eggs whisked with 4 Tablespoons hot water
1 ½ cups hot water
½ cup milk product

Beat the wet ingredients into the dry mix until the batter is smooth. It should look and feel like a thick pancake batter. This may take several minutes.

Heat a lightly oiled/ non-stick spray coated skillet or pancake griddle over medium high heat. When a drop of water sizzles and bounces off the surface, your pan is ready.

Place a large spoonful of batter into the pan and quickly spread the batter out as thin as you can. Let the chapati cook for a minute, or until firm. Flip over and cook the other side for a minute or until done. Repeat until batter is gone.

Multigrain Baguette

When I take the time to make this, it's my favorite bread for roast vegetable sandwiches.

2/3 cup sorghum flour
1/3 cup amaranth flour
½ cup millet flour
1 cup tapioca starch
2 teaspoons xanthan gum
1 ¼ teaspoon salt
2 teaspoons dry egg replacer
Sesame seeds for the top

Prepare the yeast by adding 1 Tablespoon instant dry yeast or rapid yeast to 1 ¼ cups water at 110°F, then add 1 teaspoon of any sweetener, granulated or liquid. Wait 10 minutes for the yeast to proof.

Mix together the yeast mix with 4 Tablespoons olive oil
3 Tablespoons agave nectar
½ teaspoon cider vinegar

Gently combine the dry and liquid ingredients. Knead the dough by either using a bread machine, a kitchen aid, or simply by hand. After 3 minutes, let dough rest 1 hour for rapid yeast and up to 2 hours for regular rise.

Punch down the dough and shape into a baguette. Sprinkle sesame and any other seeds/spices on top. Allow loaf to rise a second time, about 2 hours.

Preheat oven to 350°F. Grease a cookie sheet and place bread in center. Bake 30 minutes. It should sound hollow when done.

Naan

An Indian flatbread, much like pita, but traditionally made into an oblong shape. I love this with hummus or as a quick pizza.

½ cup water
2 teaspoons granulated sweetener
2 teaspoons active dry yeast
2 cups brown rice flour
½ cup potato starch
½ teaspoon salt
1 teaspoon baking powder
1 teaspoon xanthan gum
2 teaspoons vegetable oil
½ cup plain non-dairy yogurt
Egg replacer for one egg, prepared according to instructions
extra flour for flouring the surface

Preheat the oven to 450°F. Place a heavy baking tray or pizza stone in the oven to heat while you prepare the ingredients. In a measuring bowl or cup, mix water with 1 teaspoon of the sweetener and the yeast. Allow to sit in a warm place while you prep the rest of the ingredients.

Combine the flour, starch, salt, baking powder, and xanthan in a medium bowl. Add the remaining sweetener, oil, yogurt, egg replacer, and the water/yeast mixture. Blend until smooth. It will be very thick.

Divide the dough into six equal portions. Sprinkle some flour onto your rolling surface or use your hands to press the dough into a pita shape. Roll the dough until it is about ¼ " thick. Sprinkle more flour as needed onto the dough and/or the rolling pin to keep it from sticking. Bake for 6 minutes, flip and bake another 4-6 minutes until brown.

Kalamata Olive Loaf

A local bakery makes a famous Olive loaf, and I had theirs in mind.

½ cup amaranth flour
½ cup garbanzo flour
½ cup sorghum flour
1/3 cup tapioca starch
2 Tablespoons flax seed meal
3 teaspoons xanthan gum
½ cup pitted kalamata olives, chopped roughly
2 teaspoons active dry yeast
1 teaspoon salt
Egg replacer for 2 eggs, prepared according to instructions
¾ cup water, room temperature
5 Tablespoons extra virgin olive oil
2 teaspoons agave nectar
2 teaspoons apple cider vinegar

Preheat the oven to 200°F. Add the flours, yeast, and all other dry ingredients other than salt into a medium bowl. Stir in flax meal and combine.

Combine wet ingredients, including egg replacer, using a hand-mixer or stir by hand. When fully combined, add olives. Slowly add dry ingredient mixture and mix with a wooden spoon until fully blended without lumps. Try not to break the olives as you stir.

Grease a loaf pan and place dough into the pan. Use a spatula or knife to evenly shape the top of the loaf. Turn off the oven and place loaf inside. Allow the dough to rise for 90 minutes. It should rise to the very top of the pan.

Increase heat to 350°F and bake for approximately 40 minutes. The crust should be golden when done.

Sandwich Bread
An overall, basic loaf for most sandwich needs

Combine the following:

2/3 cup garbanzo flour
1/3 cup sorghum flour
½ cup tapioca starch
1 cup potato flour
2 teaspoons xanthan gum
1 ¼ teaspoons salt
2 teaspoons dry egg replacer

Prepare the yeast by adding 1 teaspoon granulated sweetener to 1 Tablespoon instant dry yeast- or rapid yeast to1 ¼ cups warm water at 110°F. Wait 10 minutes until it foams before proceeding.

Pour the liquid ingredients into the dry mix. Add:
3 Tablespoons oil
3 Tablespoons agave nectar
½ teaspoon cider vinegar

Stir to combine ingredients, then knead for a few minutes. Allow to rise 1 hour for rapid yeast and up to 2 hours for regular rise.

After waiting the 1-2 hours, shape dough into loaf shape and add to a greased loaf pan. Allow a second rising time, another 1-2 hours. Dough should rise to the edges of the pan.

Preheat oven to 350°F. Bake 30 minutes, or until loaf begins to brown. You can test with a toothpick, but also tap the loaf. It should sound hollow when done.

Not Rye Bread

I went through many loaves before perfecting this one!

In a large bowl, combine:
½ cup sorghum flour
1 cup garbanzo starch
1 cup potato flour
2 teaspoons xanthan gum
1 ¼ teaspoons salt
2 Tablespoons unsweetened cocoa powder
2 teaspoons caraway seeds
1 teaspoon minced dried onion

In a separate smaller bowl, prepare your yeast by adding 1 Tablespoon active dry yeast to 1 ¼ cups warm water at 110°F and a teaspoon of granulated or liquid sweetener. Allow the yeast to foam, about 10 minutes or so.

When the yeast is ready add:
3 Tablespoons oil
1 teaspoon cider vinegar
2 Tablespoons molasses
1 egg replacer portion for one egg, prepared according to package instructions

Pour this blend into the flour mixture and stir until a dough forms. Knead by hand or use a bread machine or mixer for 2-3 minutes. If the dough seems dry add more warm water a Tablespoon at a time. Cover and let rest for 2 hours to rise.

After rising, punch down dough and knead again. Shape into the type of loaf you want and allow a second rising time, up to 2 hours, or until the bread approximately doubles. Preheat oven to 350°F. Bake 30 minutes, and test for doneness by thumping loaf.

Oat Bread

1 ½ cups gluten-free oat flour (or quinoa if needed)
¾ cup millet flour
½ cup potato starch
1/3 cup cornstarch
1/3 cup rice flour
¼ flax seed meal
1 Tablespoon xanthan gum
Egg replacer for 3 eggs, prepared according to box package
1 teaspoon apple cider vinegar
1 packet active dry yeast
1 teaspoon desired sweetener for proofing yeast
1 Tablespoon molasses
3 Tablespoons agave nectar or other sweetener
1 ½ teaspoons salt
4 Tablespoons melted vegan butter
1 ¼ cups water at 110°F

Grease the bottom of a 10 inch loaf pan. Heat the oven to 200°F and then turn off. Sift together the dry ingredients.

In a separate medium bowl, mix egg replacer, molasses, vinegar, and melted butter together. Heat your water for preparing the yeast.

Stir together yeast and one teaspoon of sweetener. Add ¼ cup of the water to the yeast mixture. Let the yeast sit for 10 minutes.

Once your yeast is ready, add the egg mixture to the dry ingredients, then add the yeast mixture. Slowly add your water to achieve the right consistency.

Put the dough in your pan and place in oven to rise for about 2 hours. Once the dough has risen to the top of the pan, bake the bread for 40 minutes at 350°F.

About the Author

Dawn Grey, PhD, is a Certified Holistic Health Practitioner and owner of the Aruna Center of Lawrence, Kansas. After discovering in 2001 that her lifelong health issues were caused by dairy, egg, and wheat sensitivities, she changed her diet and the scope of her consultation business to help others identify and manage their own sensitivities. Now, ten years later, she is healthier, leaner, and happier than ever before.

Dawn is available for personal wellness coaching by special appointment. For more information about being a distance client of the Aruna Center, please contact Dawn at **reikirays@yahoo.com**

For additional holistic and metaphysical services, please visit her website at **www.arunacenter.com**

In addition to this cookbook, Dawn is the author of four other cookbooks: *"New Dawn Kitchen: Gluten-Free, Vegan, and Easily Sugar-Free Desserts", "The Virtuous Vegan", "The Gluten-Free Vegan Italian", and 'Cinco de Vegan"*. She is also the author of *"Reading the Tarot"* and *"The Complete Usui Reiki Guide"*.

For those interested in learning more about holistic and natural methods of healing, Dawn and her staff over accredited distance education courses at **www.reikiraysinstitute.com.**

Visit **www.newdawnkitchen.com** for more information about her cookbooks and related services.

17462487R00061

Made in the USA
Middletown, DE
25 January 2015